GIANTS OF THE OLD TESTAMENT

LESSONS ON LIVING FROM
RUTH

A devotional by
WOODROW KROLL

BACK TO THE BIBLE
Publishing

RUTH
by Back to the Bible Publishing
©1998 by Woodrow Kroll

International Standard Book Number
0-8474-0688-1

Edited by Rachel Derowitsch
Cover design by Robert Greuter
& Associates

For information:
BACK TO THE BIBLE
POST OFFICE BOX 82808
LINCOLN, NEBRASKA 68501

1 2 3 4 5 6 7 8—04 03 02 01 00 99 98

Printed in the USA

CONTENTS

DAY 1

Ruth 1:1

Now it came to pass, in the days when the judges ruled, that there was a famine in the land. And a certain man of Bethlehem, Judah, went to sojourn in the country of Moab, he and his wife and his two sons.

Desperate Times

Desperation can drive us to many extremes. Comedian Woody Allen characterized our times when he said, "We stand at a crossroads. Down one road is despondency and despair, and down the other is total annihilation. Let us pray that we choose the right road." This kind of desperation sometimes even plagues God's people and causes them to make poor choices.

Elimelech was facing desperate times, and he needed to make some difficult choices. He was struggling to feed his family. A wife and two growing boys needed nourishment, but a famine gripped the land. Famines were often God's way of bringing His people to the point of submission. They were not simply to punish Israel, but to get them to turn from their sins. Yet without clear guidance from God, Elimelech chose to run away. Instead of facing the Lord's judgment on the land and trusting God to provide, he

4

moved his family to a pagan land and raised his children in a society that did not know the God of Israel. He even broke God's law by allowing his sons to marry pagan wives (Deut. 7:3-4).

It is very tempting to look for the easy way out of our problems. But any choice that takes us away from God is, in the long run, the wrong way. Elimelech's choice ultimately brought death to himself and his two sons. No matter how desperate the situation, it is always better to face what God has allowed and trust Him than it is to run from our circumstances and go it alone.

If you are experiencing difficult times, make your choices based on clear direction from God. Don't allow a feeling of desperation to steer you in the wrong direction.

Desperate choices are seldom the best choices.

Reflections/Prayer Requests

_____

_____

_____

_____

_____

_____

DAY 2

Ruth 1:2-4

*The name of the man was Elimelech, the
name of his wife was Naomi, and the names
of his two sons were Mahlon and
Chilion—Ephrathites of Bethlehem, Judah.
And they went to the country of Moab and
remained there. Then Elimelech, Naomi's husband, died; and she was left, and her two
sons. Now they took wives of the women of
Moab: the name of the one was Orpah, and
the name of the other Ruth. And they dwelt
there about ten years.*

Transient or Tenant?

Time has a way of slipping by quickly.
Perhaps you've heard of the fellow who
said, "You know, I'm 56. I'm middle-
aged!" His wife brought him back to reality when she replied, "How many men do
you know who are 112?"

Time slipped by for the family of Elimelech as well. Ruth 1:1 indicates that Elimelech moved his family to Moab with the
intent to "sojourn" there. The word
sojourn carries the idea of a temporary
stay. Elimelech hadn't intended to remain
in the land—only to visit a short time until
the famine was over. But verse 4 reveals
that before they knew it, they had been in
the land for ten years. The sons who had
gone there as young men had grown up,

married local women and eventually passed away, as had their father (v. 5).

Sometimes we intend for situations to be only temporary. We think, *Just as soon as the kids are through college, we'll start tithing again.* Or perhaps you reason, *As soon as I get through this busy period at work, I'll get back to having a daily quiet time.* But days turn into weeks, weeks into months and before you know it, circumstances that were only going to be temporary have become a way of life.

Have you allowed something that was intended as transient to become a permanent fixture in your life? Have you been waiting for a more convenient time to do what you know you should be doing now? If time has slipped away for you, don't linger another day "in a distant land." If you're not where you should be, this is the day to do something about it.

Don't expect time to stand still just because you do.

Reflections/Prayer Requests

_____

_____

_____

_____

_____

_____

DAY 3

Ruth 1:3, 5

*Then Elimelech, Naomi's husband, died;
and she was left, and her two sons.*

*Then both Mahlon and Chilion also died;
so the woman survived her two sons
and her husband.*

Never Alone

A man took his elderly mother out to the cemetery to decorate graves for Memorial Day. After placing a bouquet of flowers on her husband's grave, she wandered among the other gravestones marking the resting places of other family members who had gone to be with the Lord. Finally she stopped, looked her son in the eye and with a wistful smile asked, "What have I done to deserve all this overtime?"

Perhaps Naomi felt the same way. She had left Israel with a husband and two sons; now only she was left—alone, and yet not alone. God had brought into her life two compassionate daughters-in-law, one of whom would follow her all the way back to Israel. Even though Naomi intensely felt the loss of her loved ones, God had not deserted her. He provided, even in a foreign land, those who would love and care for a forlorn widow.

God never really leaves us alone. When He removes those whom we expect to love and support us, He always provides another way for this need to be met. While you may experience the pain of separation, you never need to feel totally abandoned. Sometimes God grants you an unmistakable sense of His company. Other times He uses people around you to be the instruments of His love and comfort. In either case, His compassion never fails and His presence never falters.

Perhaps you have lost the one dearest to you. Maybe you have moved far away from family and friends. Let God fill your life with His presence in whatever way He chooses, and rejoice that He never forgets nor forsakes. Be assured that even though there may be an empty place in your home, there can be a fullness in your heart.

You may feel lonely, but you need never feel alone.

Reflections/Prayer Requests

_____

_____

_____

_____

_____

DAY 4

Ruth 1:6

*Then she arose with her daughters-in-law that she might return from the country of Moab, for she had heard in the country of Moab that the L*ORD *had visited His people by giving them bread.*

Heading Home

A Christian man took his eyes off God and committed a crime. He was arrested and served a seven-year sentence in a penal institution. Through an encounter with a Barnabas-like pastor, however, this man was led to know the restorative power of the blood of Jesus Christ. On the flyleaf of his Bible he wrote, "The soul that comes to Jesus through failure, shame, or pain, by His wondrous love and mercy may soar as high again."

The famine that God sent on Israel had brought a great deal of pain. It had been the primary motivation for Elimelech and his family to migrate to Moab. But for those who remained in the land, this tribulation apparently accomplished its purpose. The people repented of their sins and turned to God. For His part, God graciously restored their food supply. As the reports of Israel's recovery reached Moab, Naomi's desire was turned back toward her homeland. Although God still had work to do in her heart, this decision was the first step in her restoration to Him.

When we have sinned and turned our backs on God, the Lord often sends chastening events into our lives. As our hearts are brought to the breaking point, we sometimes wonder if God will receive us back. Is it possible for someone who has dwelt in a distant land for many years to come home again? The answer is always yes. Even though our sins are like scarlet, they can be washed white as snow (Isa. 1:18).

Have you wandered away from God? Have you been away too long? Do you fear what His response will be if you return to Him? Take heart. Jesus said, "The one who comes to Me I will by no means cast out" (John 6:37). Confess your sins, place them under the blood of Christ, and turn yourself toward home.

Repentant sinners always find God has the welcome mat out.

Reflections/Prayer Requests

_____

_____

_____

_____

_____

_____

DAY 5

Ruth 1:8

*And Naomi said to her two daughters-in-law,
"Go, return each to her mother's house. The
L*ORD* deal kindly with you, as you have dealt
with the dead and with me."*

Thy Lovingkindness

The great American novelist Henry
James, in saying good-bye to his nephew,
Willie, said something the boy never for-
got. As they parted, he put his hand on the
young man's shoulders and remarked,
"Willie, there are three things that are
important in human life. The first is to be
kind. The second is to be kind. The third is
to be kind."

Naomi's daughters-in-law, Orpah and
Ruth, apparently had learned that lesson
well. As she prepared to part from them,
Naomi praised them both for their kindness. They had been kind to her sons,
their husbands. And even after they were
widowed and no longer had family oblig-
ations to their mother-in-law, they continued to show kindness to her. In the midst
of a pagan land that practiced a cruel form
of worship—even sacrificing little children—God had so moved on the hearts of
these two women that their spirit of kindness set them apart from their fellow
Moabites.

Kindness should be one of the distinguishing marks of a Christian as well. Frederick W. Faber observed, "Kind words are the music of the world. They have a power that seems to be beyond natural causes, as if they were some angel's song that had lost its way and come to earth. It seems as if they could almost do what in reality God alone can do—soften the hard and angry hearts of men. No one was ever corrected by a sarcasm—crushed, perhaps, if the sarcasm was clever enough, but drawn nearer to God, never." We must never forget that more people have been won to Christ through kindness than fiery sermons or learned arguments.

Who needs to feel the warmth of your kindness today? Do you know someone who has a special need that you can meet? Let your life be set apart by your deeds of kindness. Identify a need. Picture a face. And show your kindness to that person today.

Kindness is love in work clothes.

Reflections/Prayer Requests

_____

_____

_____

_____

_____

DAY 6

Ruth 1:11

But Naomi said, "Turn back, my daughters; why will you go with me? Are there still sons in my womb, that they may be your husbands?"

So Right, Yet So Wrong

When Egypt first conquered a land called Nubia, a regiment of soldiers was sent across the desert with an Arab guide. The men suffered extreme thirst. Suddenly, they saw a lake in the distance. It seemed logical to head right for the lake. Although their guide assured them the lake was not real, the soldiers were convinced that it was. It had to be; they could see it. The soldiers decided to kill the guide and then set out to reach the lake. But to their dismay, the water turned out to be only a mirage. Every soldier perished.

What seems logical isn't necessarily right. Naomi presented a very logical argument. It was not possible for her to bear sons to replace Mahlon and Chilion; and even if she could, Orpah and Ruth would not want to wait until these boys were old enough to marry. The obvious conclusion was that her daughters-in-law should return to their Moabite families. That sounded reasonable, so Orpah did.

As a result, though, she eventually perished without knowing the God of Israel. Ruth, on the other hand, rejected the logical argument and ultimately found herself drawn into the family of God.

God often doesn't follow the dictates of human logic. That doesn't mean He's illogical, but that His logic transcends ours. The way God does things is not always the way we do things (Isa. 55:8-9). While we are limited in knowledge and power, God is omniscient and omnipotent. While we are trapped in time and space, God is eternal and omnipresent. Our logic reflects our limitations; God's logic reflects His unlimited ability.

Take care when following human reasoning—it may seem right at the time, but "its end is the way of death" (Prov. 14:12). Always trust God's logic; it's the way of life. To know God's logic you must know His will, and to know God's will you must read His Word. That's where you must begin today.

Logic is only as good as its source.

Reflections/Prayer Requests

_____

_____

_____

_____

DAY 7

Ruth 1:14

Then they lifted up their voices and wept again; and Orpah kissed her mother-in-law, but Ruth clung to her.

Super-glued

A number of years ago a new glue, characterized by an unusually strong holding power, was introduced on the market and sold under a variety of names. Advertisements for this product showed such unusual feats as a car being lifted with a crane while attached only by means of this glue. On another occasion, a full-grown elephant was lifted into the air after having its harness glued to a hoist. The message came through clearly: this super glue bonds in an extraordinary way.

That's the way Ruth bonded to Naomi. Certainly her old life had a pull on Ruth's heart. She was not insensitive to her old customs, her familiar haunts or her Moabite family. But the glue that bound her spirit to Naomi was even stronger. It simply would not let go. She "clung" to her mother-in-law with the tenacity of a super glue. Ruth was committed to a whole new life, not just a change of jobs or a change of scenery. Turning back and separating herself from Naomi was not an option.

This same bonding takes place when we receive Christ as our Savior. The Bible says that there is One who "sticks closer than a brother" (Prov. 18:24). The apostle Paul asks, "Who shall separate us from the love of Christ? Shall tribulation, or distress, or persecution, or famine, or nakedness, or peril, or sword?" (Rom 8:35). He answers his question a few verses later: "For I am persuaded that neither death nor life, nor angels nor principalities nor powers, nor things present nor things to come, nor height nor depth, nor any other created thing, shall be able to separate us from the love of God which is in Christ Jesus our Lord" (Rom. 8:38-39).

If you are feeling abandoned today, at loose ends with everything around you, rest in the assurance that Jesus sticks with you. Christ will cling to you with a tenacity that would put even a super glue to shame. He will never let you go.

When you're glued to Christ, you're glued for good.

Reflections/Prayer Requests

_____

_____

_____

_____

_____

DAY 8

Ruth 1:15

And she said, "Look, your sister-in-law has gone back to her people and to her gods; return after your sister-in-law."

Follow Me

Husbands are notorious for not asking directions. One wife said that her husband and she left a wedding to go to the reception. Not knowing how to find the reception hall, her husband chose to follow one of the other wedding guests rather than ask directions. After numerous twists and turns, the car ahead of them finally pulled into the driveway of their own home. As it turned out, these guests had not planned to attend the reception.

Where a person is going should influence whether or not we want to follow him. Naomi urged her daughter-in-law Ruth to follow the way Orpha, her sister-in-law, had taken. But Orpha was headed in the wrong direction. She was going back to her people and her gods. Orpha had been exposed to the God of Israel while she was a part of Elimelech's family, but when the final decision had to be made, she chose to return to her old way of life. Fortunately, Ruth chose not to accompany her.

Many people are seeking others to follow them, but they're headed in the wrong direction. When we cut through all their assurances and promises, we discover that what they're really offering is to lead us back to enslavement to the world. The apostle Paul urged the Corinthians, "Imitate me, just as I also imitate Christ" (1 Cor. 11:1). The same applies to us today. Choose to follow only those who have chosen to follow Christ.

Be careful whom you allow to be your leader. Take time today to make sure you're following someone who honors the Lord. Anyone who is not headed in the same direction as Christ is not headed in a direction you want to go.

Before you follow, know where you're being led.

Reflections/Prayer Requests

_____

_____

_____

_____

_____

_____

_____

_____

DAY 9

Ruth 1:16-17

But Ruth said: "Entreat me not to leave you, or to turn back from following after you; for wherever you go, I will go; and wherever you lodge, I will lodge; your people shall be my people, and your God, my God. Where you die, I will die, and there will I be buried. The LORD do so to me, and more also, if anything but death parts you and me."

Important Choices

A sign on the door of a classroom in a junior high school in Kansas declares, "We are not born losers, we are born choosers." How very true. Each day we are faced with choices, some of which have the potential of changing our lives forever.

Ruth faced such choices. She had to choose whether to return to her people with her sister-in-law, Orpha, or to follow Naomi, her mother-in-law. She chose her mother-in-law. She had to choose whether to identify herself as a pagan Moabite or throw her lot in with the people of Israel. She chose the people of Israel. She had to choose to worship the idol Chemosh, which involved the sacrifice of children, or to put her trust in the living God, who gives life instead of taking it. She chose Jehovah. These were impor-

20

tant choices, and she made them with a determination that changed her life.

Like Ruth, we are all born outside of God's family. But God graciously gives us the opportunity to make choices that can give us eternal life. Instead of continuing in Satan's kingdom of darkness, you can choose to change your allegiance to the kingdom of His beloved Son (Col. 1:13). You can choose to continue in the deeds of darkness or walk in the light (Eph. 5:7-10). You can choose to search for fulfillment in the world or place your trust in Jesus, who has promised to meet your every need (Phil. 4:19). Like Ruth's, these are crucial decisions and, when made with determination, can change your life.

What decisions have you made? Choose rightly. Choose life. Choose Jesus Christ as your Savior. This is the most important decision of your life.

You always choose best when you choose God.

Reflections/Prayer Requests

_____

_____

_____

_____

_____

DAY 10

Ruth 1:20-21

So she said to them, "Do not call me Naomi; call me Mara, for the Almighty has dealt very bitterly with me. I went out full, and the LORD has brought me home again empty. Why do you call me Naomi, since the LORD has testified against me, and the Almighty has afflicted me?"

Angry at God

A growing problem in the United States is "road rage." Between January 1, 1990, and September 1, 1996, the American Automobile Association counted at least 10,037 incidents of road rage resulting in 218 deaths. An additional 12,610 people were injured. This is a terrible price to pay for foolishly venting one's anger. Yet it's far more foolish when we become angry at God.

When Naomi returned to her homeland, it was obvious she was angry with God for the losses in her life. When her friends called her Naomi (which means "sweetness" or "pleasantness"), she instructed them instead to call her Mara (which means "bitterness"), because "the Almighty has afflicted me." She lamented that left Bethlehem with a husband and two sons, but returned "empty." She was angry at God because of what He had allowed.

In God's plan, however, Naomi was actually at the beginning of the most fulfilling time of her life. Soon Ruth would meet and marry Boaz and bear his child. That baby, Obed, would become the grandfather to Israel's greatest king, David, who would establish the lineage of the Messiah, Jesus. What God had allowed to be taken away from Naomi would be replaced with blessings beyond her wildest imagination.

When you experience the grief of losing a loved one—a husband, a wife, a child—it's easy to become bitter and lash out at God. You think it's all His fault. He allowed it to happen. Yet the God who loves you is also the God who sees the end from the beginning. He knows what He is doing. Trust Him. What has begun as a heartache for you will ultimately result in overwhelming blessings.

Sorrow is the garden in which God grows our blessings.

Reflections/Prayer Requests

_____

_____

_____

_____

_____

_____

DAY 11

Ruth 1:22

So Naomi returned, and Ruth the Moabitess her daughter-in-law with her, who returned from the country of Moab. Now they came to Bethlehem at the beginning of barley harvest.

Just in Time

According to *Business Week*, time technicians at the National Institute of Standards & Technology recently switched to an atomic clock based on the vibrations of cesium atoms. It will take 300,000 years to gain or lose a single second. But NIST scientists are working on an even better model: a single mercury ion will be trapped in a vacuum by laser beams and cooled to its lowest possible energy level. The atom's oscillations will then be so stable that the new timepiece should be accurate to within one second in ten billion years.

Yet God's timing is even more accurate than that. He brought Naomi and Ruth back from Moab just as the barley harvest was beginning. This had a twofold significance. By God's good timing, they returned at a season when food would be available for a destitute widow and her daughter-in-law. The law of gleaning (Lev. 19:9; 23:22) allowed the poor to follow the harvesters and gather any stray stalks of grain. In fact, the corners of the field were to be left deliberately unharvested so the less fortunate would be provided for. But it was also perfect timing because, most likely, it was only during the harvest season that Boaz regularly visited his fields. This provided an occasion for Ruth and Boaz to meet and develop a relationship.

God's timing is never off. We may get in a hurry or lag behind, but God is the Master of time. His plans always take place in the "fullness of the time" (Gal. 4:4). Never a moment too soon or a second too late, but at the appropriate time He brings about His perfect will.

Trust your time to God. He is a billion times better than an atomic clock. At the right time, He will open the way for you.

God is never in a hurry because He is in control of time.

Reflections/Prayer Requests

_____

_____

_____

_____

_____

_____

_____

DAY 12

Ruth 2:1

And Naomi had a kinsman of her husband's, a man of great wealth, of the family of Elimelech; his name was Boaz.

Real Riches

John Jacob Astor, one of the world's richest men, was a passenger on the ill-fated maiden voyage of the *Titanic*. When the ship hit the iceberg and it turned out that there was a shortage of lifeboats, the multimillionaire gave up his chance for safety and went down with the ship. His body was eventually found dressed in a blue suit, with $2,500 in his pocket. But on that fateful night, as he faced eternity, it mattered little what he possessed.

God provided a rich relative for Ruth who had more than possessions; Boaz had honor as well. The word translated "wealth" in Ruth 2:1 is often translated "might" or "valor" in the Bible. It reflects Boaz's strength of character as much as his financial portfolio. He not only had land and houses, but he also was a man of spiritual valor, a mighty man of integrity, an upright man who had placed his trust in God.

God wants all His children to be rich—but not necessarily in material possessions. When the apostle Paul reached the end of his life, all he owned was an extra cloak and some books (2 Tim. 4:13). Barnabas sold his land and gave the money to the needy (Acts 4:34-37). But these men weren't really paupers. In their poverty, they had a richness of peace and joy that many who are wealthy only dream about.

What keeps you up at night? Worry over your stocks and bonds, or agonizing over the souls of those who are lost? What are you striving for? Material wealth that will one day be left behind, or a spiritual wealth that will last for eternity? Make the right choice and then set the right priorities.

If all you have is money, then you have nothing at all.

Reflections/Prayer Requests

_____

_____

_____

_____

_____

_____

_____

_____

_____

_____

DAY 13

Ruth 2:2

So Ruth the Moabitess said to Naomi,
"Please let me go to the field, and glean
heads of grain after him in whose sight
I may find favor." And she said to her,
"Go, my daughter."

Finding Favor

Sometimes we try to buy people's favor—and even God's favor. We're like the little girl who won five dollars for her memory work in Sunday school. Later when the pastor's wife congratulated her, the girl proudly announced, "And I put it all in the morning's offering!" "My, how wonderful!" the pastor's wife exclaimed. "I'm sure God will be pleased." "Yes," the child replied, "now maybe He will let me do some of the things I want to do!" This little girl was looking for the wrong kind of favor in the wrong place.

Ruth was also looking for favor—but not the kind you buy with money or flattery. She wanted to come by her favor honestly. She trusted God to bring her to someone's field who would accept her as she was. Even though she wasn't an Israelite, she hoped someone would allow her to glean what was left in the fields. The favor she sought would be the result of the gleaner's grace, not Ruth's glory.

This is the kind of favor God offers. Nothing we possess or do can influence Him to look with favor on us. We cannot buy His favor or manipulate Him by our behavior. His favor comes because He loves us, even while we are yet sinners (Rom. 5:8). Through His Son, Jesus Christ, God has made it possible for our sins to be forgiven (Eph. 1:7). God's favor is given because of who He is, not because of who we are.

Have you found favor in God's sight? You can, right now, right where you are, by confessing that you are a sinner and asking Jesus Christ to be your Savior.

God's favor can be neither bought nor sold, but it can be enjoyed.

Reflections/Prayer Requests

_____

_____

_____

_____

_____

_____

_____

_____

_____

_____

DAY 14

Ruth 2:5-6

Then Boaz said to his servant who was in charge of the reapers, "Whose young woman is this?" So the servant who was in charge of the reapers answered and said, "It is the young Moabite woman who came back with Naomi from the country of Moab."

Not by Chance

Nothing happens by chance. Take, for example, the blue whale. Longer than three dump trucks, heavier than 110 Honda Civics and with a heart the size of a Volkswagen Beetle, this magnificent creature requires four tons of krill a day (that's three million calories) for its sustenance. Even a baby blue whale can put away 100 gallons of milk every 24 hours. When a blue whale surfaces, it takes in the largest breath of air of any living thing on the planet. Its spray shoots higher into the air than the height of a telephone pole. How did such a creature come into existence? Not by chance, you can be sure, but by a sovereign Creator's plan.

Neither did Boaz by chance come to his fields just in time to meet Ruth. He certainly didn't come with any intentions of finding a wife, but that was God's plan. Ruth, too, was simply doing what she needed to do for survival. In fact, until she spoke with Naomi, she wasn't even aware of Boaz's relationship with the family she had married into (2:19-20). But in God's plans nothing happens by chance.

Sometimes our circumstances seem to come about by chance. We think, *If I had made this decision instead of that decision, my life would be different.* Or, *If I'd been here instead of there, this wouldn't have happened.* While we cannot use this as an excuse for making poor decisions, we can have the confidence that nothing happens by chance. Take care of your responsibilities in a way that honors God, and He will work out His plan through you.

If you are struggling with the "what ifs" of life, put them aside. Be assured that God is working out His plan for you, and it won't be by chance.

Since God is in charge, nothing is by chance.

Reflections/Prayer Requests

_____

_____

_____

_____

_____

DAY 15

Ruth 2:7

*"And she said, 'Please let me glean
and gather after the reapers among the
sheaves.' So she came and has continued
from morning until now, though she rested
a little in the house."*

No Free Lunches

There's a delightful story about a king,
many years ago, who called his wise men
together and gave them this commission:
"I want you to compile for me the wisdom
of the ages and put it in book form so we
can leave it to posterity." The men left the
king and worked hard. Sometime later
they returned with 12 volumes. The king
looked at the imposing volumes and said,
"It's too long and I fear people will not
read it. Condense it!" Still later the wise
men returned with only one volume.
Again the king said, "Condense it." They
then reduced the volume to a chapter,
then to a page, then to a paragraph and
finally to a sentence. When the king saw
the sentence, elatedly he announced.
"Gentlemen, this is truly the wisdom of the
ages." The sentence simply said, "There
are no free lunches."

Ruth recognized that sage truth as
well. She did not wait for someone to
come along with a handout; instead, she

worked from "morning until now." She was diligent in her labors and made a very favorable impression on the other harvesters.

God expects those who bear the name of Christ to honor Him through their work. Paul taught that "if anyone will not work, neither shall he eat" (2 Thess. 3:10). He also reminded the Christians at Thessalonica, "Nor did we eat anyone's bread free of charge, but worked with labor and toil night and day, that we might not be a burden to any of you" (v. 8). A slacker is not only a disgrace to himself, but he brings shame upon the Lord as well.

Consider your job a blessing, not a burden. No matter how menial it might seem, see your work as an outlet to honor the Lord. Approach it every day with enthusiasm and dedication. After all, even the ability to work for a living is a gift from God (Eccl. 5:18-19).

Work can be worship when you do it for God.

Reflections/Prayer Requests

_____

_____

_____

_____

DAY 16

Ruth 2:8

*Then Boaz said to Ruth, "You will listen, my
daughter, will you not? Do not go to glean in
another field, nor go from here, but stay close
by my young women."*

Bite by Bite

Nebraska, where I live, has a lot of cattle ranches, and every once in a while a cow wanders off and gets lost. If you were to ask a rancher how a cow gets lost, chances are he would reply, "Well, the cow starts nibbling on a tuft of green grass, and when it finishes, it looks ahead to the next tuft of green grass. After it finishes that one, it looks ahead and starts nibbling on the next one, and then it nibbles on some grass right next to a hole in the fence. When it sees another tuft of green grass on the other side of the fence, it nibbles on that one and then another one—and the next thing you know, the cow has nibbled itself lost."

Boaz knew how easy it was to drift into danger. His fear for Ruth was that she might wander into the field of some unscrupulous person who would take advantage of her. Therefore he admonished her, "Stay close by my young women." In other words, don't stray from the company of my female workers and you'll be safe.

34

Sin works on the same principle. Seldom does Satan open a big hole in the fence for us to dash through into sin. He always begins by tempting us with a little "tuft of sin," and that's followed by a bit bigger one, and another one, until we lift our heads and realize we have nibbled ourselves far from God. Bite by bite, we have wandered away until we're lost.

If you find yourself in that situation today, do two things. Stop right were you are and look around to see where God is. Then, take comfort. The One who loves you more than anything else in the world has come to "seek and to save that which was lost" (Luke 19:10). Admit that you have wandered and confess that you have sinned, and He will help you find your way home again.

Be careful where you take the next bite.

Reflections/Prayer Requests

_____

_____

_____

_____

_____

_____

_____

DAY 17

Ruth 2:9

"Let your eyes be on the field which they reap, and go after them. Have I not commanded the young men not to touch you? And when you are thirsty, go to the vessels and drink from what the young men have drawn."

Divine Protection

An Alpine mountain climbing team came to a perilous gap in the ice. The only way to get across was to step into the out-stretched hands of the guide who had met them on the other side. The first climber hesitated a moment as he looked into the gloomy depths below, where he would certainly fall to his death if anything went wrong. Seeing his hesitancy, the guide said, "Don't worry. In all my years as a guide, my hands have never yet lost a man!"

With this same assurance, Ruth placed herself in Boaz's hands. God provided someone who would protect her. Boaz took steps to keep her morally safe by commanding the young men not to touch her. He also provided for her physical protection. Under the hot Mediterranean sun, the danger of heat stroke was a very real possibility. But his young men brought jars of water to the field, and Ruth was free to refresh herself whenever she wanted. In Boaz, Ruth found a safe haven from the dangers around her.

God offers the same to all His children. There is never a moment when we are excluded from His divine protection. That does not mean we can never be hurt. It doesn't mean we will never die. But God's divine protection extends to our ultimate safety—the protection of our souls. These can never be harmed. They are safe in the care of Jesus.

Rejoice in God's divine protection. Be confident that you are safe in His care, no matter how difficult your circumstances might be. God is the keeper of your soul.

Life can hurt us but it cannot ultimately harm us.

Reflections/Prayer Requests

_____

_____

_____

_____

_____

_____

_____

_____

DAY 18

Ruth 2:10-11

*So she fell on her face, bowed down
to the ground, and said to him, "Why have
I found favor in your eyes, that you should
take notice of me, since I am a foreigner?"
And Boaz answered and said to her, "It has
been fully reported to me, all that you have
done for your mother-in-law since the death
of your husband, and how you have left
your father and your mother and the land
of your birth, and have come to a people
whom you did not know before."*

A Good Report

When Jim Wright, the former speaker of the House, resigned, he quoted Horace Greeley: "Fame is a vapor, popularity an accident, riches take wings, those who cheer today may curse tomorrow; only one thing endures—character."

When Boaz justified his kindness toward Ruth, he did not say that he had heard of her great beauty or her brilliant intellect. No mention is ever made of these things. But what spoke volumes to Boaz was what he had heard about Ruth's character. He had heard about her relationship with Naomi and Ruth's willingness to leave her own family and country in order to take care of her widowed mother-in-law—even though she was a widow herself. It's not surprising that

Boaz was impressed with Ruth. He knew that a woman with this kind of character was rare and precious.

God is not interested in our fame or fortune; He cares nothing for our popularity or wealth. What God cares about is our character. The trials that He allows to come into our lives—even the loss of loved ones, as Ruth experienced—are for the ultimate perfection of our character.

What do people hear about you? Do you try to impress others with your financial portfolio, your athletic abilities or your great intellect? These are all gifts from God, so where's the brag factor? What about your character? That's what God is looking for in us. Strive to be known for what you are, not what you do. Character counts.

Concentrate on your character; everything else will take care of itself.

Reflections/Prayer Requests

_____

_____

_____

_____

_____

_____

_____

DAY 19

Ruth 2:12

"The LORD repay your work, and a full reward be given you by the LORD God of Israel, under whose wings you have come for refuge."

Under His Wings

Birds use their wings for many purposes other than flying. In times of danger, a mother bird's wings provide a feathered canopy of protection. When darkness falls and the temperature drops, it is under their mother's wings that young chicks find the warmth they need to make it through the frosty night. As the rain plummets to the earth, these same wings provide dry shelter. For those who are young and vulnerable, the wings of their mother promise the safety and security they need.

This is the safety and security Boaz alluded to as he assured Ruth that her kind and unselfish deeds would not go unrewarded. When she abandoned the security of her homeland to care for her mother-in-law, Naomi, Ruth may have wondered about her future. She had left everything that spelled safety, but she found something even greater—a refuge that exists only under the wings of the God of Israel. The word translated "refuge" means "to flee for protection."

Under the shelter of God's wings, Ruth found the protection she needed.

God never abandons His own. In times of danger and distress, He spreads His wings of protection and comfort over us. Enveloped by His pinions, we do not need to fear the difficult circumstances of life. Personal storms may rage around us, but we are safe under the canopy of God's constant care. The psalmist assures us, "He shall cover you with His feathers, and under His wings you shall take refuge" (Ps. 91:4).

If you are going through painful times, nestle yourself under His wings. Take comfort in the fact that God's protection is spread over you. Nothing can touch your life without His express permission. Nothing can threaten you without His express protection.

God's protection is more than a match for our problems.

Reflections/Prayer Requests

_____

_____

_____

_____

_____

_____

DAY 20

Ruth 2:14

Now Boaz said to her at mealtime, "Come here, and eat of the bread, and dip your piece of bread in the vinegar." So she sat beside the reapers, and he passed parched grain to her; and she ate and was satisfied, and kept some back.

More Than Enough

In 1949, Mr. Jack Wurm was broke and out of a job. One day as he walked along a San Francisco beach, he came across a bottle with a piece of paper in it. The note was the last will and testament of Daisy Singer Alexander, heir to the Singer sewing machine fortune. It read, "To avoid confusion, I leave my entire estate to the lucky person who finds this bottle and to my attorney, Barry Cohen. Share and share alike." In one fell swoop, Mr. Wurm was transformed from a penniless indigent to the possessor of over $6 million dollars in cash and Singer stock. Suddenly, he had more than enough.

Ruth experienced the same. As a destitute widow, she hoped to glean enough barley to provide a few morsels of food for herself and Naomi. Suddenly, because of the kindness of Boaz, she had enough to eat and even some to take home to her mother-in-law. She moved from bare necessities to an abundance she could never have dreamed of.

When we encounter Christ, the same is true for us. We come to him with nothing to offer. Isaiah says that "all our righteousnesses are like filthy rags" (Isa. 64:6). We are morally broken and spiritually bankrupt. However, in a moment of time, as we open our hearts to receive the Lord, we are forever changed. We are washed clean, and we are filled to overflowing with the eternal riches of Christ. We are changed from spiritual paupers to coheirs with Christ.

Don't count your wealth in terms of dollars and cents. As a child of the King, you have more than enough to be forever satisfied.

Only One who is Himself more than enough can truly satisfy.

Reflections/Prayer Requests

_____

_____

_____

_____

_____

_____

_____

DAY 21

Ruth 2:22-23

*And Naomi said to Ruth her daughter-in-law,
"It is good, my daughter, that you go out with
his young women, and that people do not
meet you in any other field." So she stayed
close by the young women of Boaz, to glean
until the end of barley harvest and wheat harvest; and she dwelt with her mother-in-law.*

Abide With Me

When travelers visit a foreign land,
they are often issued a visa. A visa, in
essence, is an agreement with that gov-
ernment that you will stay no longer than
a set number of days or months. If that
time expires, you must either renew your
visa or leave the country. A visa is not for
those who plan to live in a country; it's
only for those who plan to visit.

Ruth did not have a visa. When she followed Naomi back to Israel, she had no
intention of ever returning to Moab. The
Bible says she "dwelt" with her mother-in-
law. This verb implies establishing a permanent residence. She was not just there
for a visit; she was there for good.

When we come to Christ, it should be
with the idea of taking up permanent residence. We do not come to sample the
weather and see if we like it. Having tried
everything else, we don't "try Jesus."

44

Instead, we come as those ready to sur-render allegiance to all other "countries" and to make Jesus our permanent home. Jesus said, "Abide in Me, and I in you" (John 15:4). The consistency and perma-nency about our relationship set it apart from a mere visit. Furthermore, this com-mitment is reciprocated as Jesus promises to do the same for us. He abides in us, as we abide in Him. Only then can we bear much fruit for God's glory (v. 5).

Do you want to enjoy life to the fullest? Then walk consistently with Christ. Be regular in your prayer times and Bible reading. Be faithful to your local church. Let it be obvious that you're not a visitor, but have taken up residence in Christ.

Those who abide in Christ don't need a visa for heaven.

Reflections/Prayer Requests

_____

_____

_____

_____

_____

_____

_____

_____

DAY 22

Ruth 3:4

"Then it shall be, when he lies down, that you shall notice the place where he lies; and you shall go in, uncover his feet, and lie down; and he will tell you what you should do."

Waiting for Instructions

A few years ago, a $100,000 mistake was made because someone failed to wait for complete instructions. As reported in *Entrepreneur* magazine, a dispatcher for a cement company was instructed to send a fleet of trucks to Portland. For some reason he failed to wait for the rest of the message. The result: eight trucks of cement went to Portland, Oregon, when their real destination was 3,000 miles away in Portland, Maine.

Naomi wisely cautioned Ruth to wait for instructions—complete instructions. Ruth was to approach Boaz after the festivities at the threshing floor. Uncovering his feet was not an improper flirtation. As a Middle Eastern custom, it was a way for a woman to ask that she be taken into the man's family as his wife. There was nothing improper here. Afterwards, Naomi prudently advised her, "Don't hurry. Don't try to second-guess what Boaz might have to say. Simply wait, 'and he will tell you what you should do.'"

God also promises to give us complete instructions. The psalmist said of the Lord, "I will instruct you and teach you in the way you should go; I will guide you with My eye" (Ps. 32:8). The God who knows the beginning from the end, who holds the past, present and future in His hands, wants to communicate His total plan for our lives. But it seldom comes all at one time. Instead, God reveals a little bit, and then we wait. He reveals a little more, and again we wait. But through this process, we become aware of God's complete instructions for our lives.

Are you eager to know God's plan for your life? Don't rush ahead of Him. Be patient and wait for Him to reveal His instructions. Then go only so far as He reveals. When you no longer know what God would have you do next, stop and wait for Him to tell you more. Give Him time; God will make it all clear.

Waiting for God's instructions is time well spent.

Reflections/Prayer Requests

_____

_____

_____

_____

_____

DAY 23

Ruth 3:8

Now it happened at midnight that the man was startled, and turned himself; and there, a woman was lying at his feet.

In the Dark

Most crimes take place in the dark. In the dark of the night a thief slips into a home to steal. In dimly lit parking garages assailants lurk about for their next victims. In the blackness of alleys gang members hatch their plans.

Depraved men love the darkness because it hides their wicked deeds (John 3:19). And here was a perfect opportunity—a man alone with a woman in the dark. No one would have noticed; it was midnight and everyone was sound asleep. Nor probably would they have cared, had they taken note. Ruth was a foreigner and, worse yet, a Moabitess. Since the days of Moses when Moabites refused to allow passage through their land and even hired Balaam to curse the Israelites, no love existed between these two nations. Furthermore, Boaz was wealthy, and everyone knows that the rich take what they want. But Boaz was a man of honor and integrity—even in the dark.

God expects you and me to behave in the dark the same as we do in the light. It makes no difference if no one is watching. It doesn't even matter that our misdeeds will never be discovered. There is still One who knows and cares. The psalmist reminds us, "the darkness and the light are both alike to [God]" (Ps. 139:12). The darkness is not the time to take a chance; it's the time to show your character.

Make sure God can trust you in the dark. Ask Him to give you the consistency of character that is unaffected by your circumstances. Be as faithful to the Lord when your actions are hidden as when they're out in the open. Someday, you'll be glad you did.

What a person is in the dark is what a person truly is.

Reflections/Prayer Requests

_____

_____

_____

_____

_____

_____

_____

_____

_____

_____

DAY 24

Ruth 3:11

"And now, my daughter, do not fear. I will do for you all that you request, for all the people of my town know that you are a virtuous woman."

A Virtuous Woman

Blaise Pascal, a 17th-century philosopher and theologian, declared, "The virtue of a man ought to be measured, not by his extraordinary exertions, but by his everyday conduct."

The people of Bethlehem had noticed Ruth's daily conduct, and that earned her the reputation of being a virtuous woman. She lived during the period known as the Judges, an era of Israel's history when "everyone did what was right in his own eyes" (Judg. 17:6). It was a time of loose morals, and, as she approached Boaz in the dark of night, her good intentions might have been misunderstood. But Boaz knew her reputation for virtue, and he had seen her conduct as she gleaned among the reapers. Based on this information, he had no question about her motives and no qualms in agreeing to do all that she requested.

God wants His people to live virtuous lives no matter what the rest of society does. Peter admonished, "But also for this very reason [the corruption of the world], giving all diligence, add to your faith virtue" (2 Pet. 1:5). In the midst of a society that appears to enjoy wallowing in the pigsty of immorality, it is imperative that we live with virtue. Why? Because virtuous living keeps us in close fellowship with God. In addition, it sets us apart as a witness to the cleansing power of Jesus Christ. At a time when once again "every man is doing what is right in his own eyes," you and I need to be distinguished as people of virtue.

Make sure your daily conduct reflects faith *and* virtue. In every respect, deal honestly with those around you. Keep not only your actions but also your thoughts from impurity. By doing so, you'll build for yourself the best reputation of all—not of shrewdness or business acumen, but of virtue.

A life without virtue is a life without value.

Reflections/Prayer Requests

_____

_____

_____

_____

_____

_____

DAY 25

Ruth 3:17

And she said, "These six ephahs of barley he gave me; for he said to me, 'Do not go empty-handed to your mother-in-law.'"

Do Not Go Empty-handed

Recently the Barna Research Group announced its findings that the number of evangelicals in the United States is only about 6 percent (decreasing from 12 percent in 1992). An earlier study indicated that as many as 40 percent of Americans have no religious affiliation and another 31 percent are Christians in name only. That means that at least 71 percent of the U.S. population are living in spiritual poverty. It's obvious we have a vast mission field right in our own backyard. As we send and support missionaries overseas, are we overlooking those in spiritual need nearby?

Many people in Israel lived in physical poverty, and Boaz was known for his generosity. But in his concern for those elsewhere, he didn't overlook those in need in his own backyard. One of those was his own kinswoman, Naomi. As Ruth prepared to go home from her labors in the field, he gave her six ephahs (approximately five bushels) of barley to take home to her mother-in-law. Out of the compassion of his heart, he was burdened that the young Moabitess who gleaned in his fields not go home empty-handed.

Spiritually needy people are everywhere. The majority of Christians, however, are neither able nor called to leave their occupations and homes to serve on foreign mission fields. But that doesn't mean that our neighbors must go home empty-handed. All around us are people living well below the "spiritual poverty line." Next door, around the corner or in the apartment across the hall are men, women and children who need to know about the Savior. The fields are there, and they're ready for harvest.

Make sure your friends and neighbors don't go home empty-handed. Be alert to opportunities to pass on the Bread of Life. Prayerfully ask God to lead you to someone with whom you can share your spiritual bounty. And then be like Boaz: give away what your friends need most.

If you're content to go to heaven alone, you may not be going at all.

Reflections/Prayer Requests

_____

_____

_____

_____

DAY 26

Ruth 3:18

Then she said, "Sit still, my daughter, until you know how the matter will turn out; for the man will not rest until he has concluded the matter this day."

Sit Still

American culture is built around the oft-quoted phrase, "Don't just stand there, do something!" As a result, our lives are filled with busyness. We rush from meeting to meeting. We chauffeur our children from hockey practice to tennis lessons to shopping at the mall. We pull in to the nearest fast-food drive-through, place a quick order, and then we're off again. It's no wonder we can identify with Blaise Pascal, who said, "All the troubles of life come upon us because we refuse to sit quietly."

Naomi knew better. Her advice—sit still, stay quiet—was filled with the wisdom of experience. Ruth had come to Naomi and told her all that took place at the threshing floor. It was obvious to Naomi that God was at work. How things were going to turn out, however, she didn't know. But she did know that this was not the time to rush here and there to find the answer. Instead, it was the time to sit quietly and listen intently for the Lord's response. At the right time, God would bring everything to pass.

When much is at stake, do you have difficulty sitting still? If you will remember to wait patiently, you will see a number of positive things happen. In stillness you'll discover God in new and deeper ways (Ps. 46:10). You'll also be able to hear God when He speaks to you in a still, small voice (1 Kings 19:12). Furthermore, you'll have the wisdom and strength to act when the time is right (Isa. 30:15).

Sit still and let God work in your life. Trust Him to accomplish what is best for you in His own timing. Listen quietly and you will hear His answer.

While you rest, God will work.

Reflections/Prayer Requests

DAY 27

Ruth 4:5-6

*Then Boaz said, "On the day you buy
the field from the hand of Naomi,
you must also buy it from Ruth the Moabitess,
the wife of the dead, to raise up the name
of the dead on his inheritance." And the near
kinsman said, "I cannot redeem it for myself,
lest I ruin my own inheritance. You redeem
my right of redemption for yourself,
for I cannot redeem it."*

Nearsighted

Myopia is an eye condition in which visual images come into focus in front of the retina, causing distant objects to be blurred. We commonly call this being nearsighted. We can see things close up but not far away.

People also can be nearsighted in their understanding of God's plan for their life. The relative who was closest to Naomi and Ruth turned down the opportunity to redeem Naomi's land and marry Ruth because he feared it might jeopardize his own inheritance. He could see clearly what he had; however, he failed to discern what might be in the future. He chose to protect his current possessions, and thus missed the opportunity to be the grandfather of a king and the ancestor of the Messiah. Consequently, he passed off the scene without even a mention of his name.

Many individuals today do the same. They pour everything they have into this life—all their time, talent, energy and money. Yet they fail to invest in eternity, as Jesus instructed us to do (Matt. 6:19-20). They clearly discern what they have, but they fail to see that there's something even more in store for them. They focus on the present and neglect the future. They give up all the wonders of heaven for the temporary security of earthly treasures. And when the winds of history pass, even their names are forgotten.

Don't suffer from spiritual myopia. As a good steward, take care of what God entrusts to you today. But don't let today's possessions blind you to eternity's possibilities. What lies ahead is worth far more than anything you hold in your hands today. The best is yet to come.

Don't let what is good rob you of what is best.

Reflections/Prayer Requests

_____

_____

_____

_____

_____

DAY 28

Ruth 4:9

*And Boaz said to the elders and all
the people, "You are witnesses this day
that I have bought all that was Elimelech's,
and all that was Chilion's and Mahlon's,
from the hand of Naomi."*

Twice Owned

A father and son built a toy sailboat.
Before launching it, the father tied a string
to its stern to keep it from sailing too far.
The boat performed beautifully, but before
long a motorboat crossing the lake cut the
string, and the sailboat drifted out of sight.
The boat couldn't be found anywhere. A
few weeks later the boy passed his
favorite toy store and saw his lost sailboat
in the window. He ran inside to claim it.
The store owner replied, "You may have
been its maker," he said, "but as its finder,
it now belongs to me. You may buy it back
for fifty dollars." The boy was stunned at
the cost, but he set about earning the
money.

Months later he walked into the store
and handed the owner $50. As he left the
store, he held the boat up to the sunlight.
Its colors gleamed. He mused, "I once
owned you, but I lost you. Now I've
bought you back. That makes you twice
mine.

The land that Naomi's husband owned had been lost, perhaps sold to provide food during the famine. According to Jewish law, the nearest relative to her was responsible to buy back that land if possible. Boaz agreed to be that redeemer after the nearest kinsman refused.

This is a picture of what Christ has done for us. As our Creator, He made us and owned us, but by our rebellion we sold ourselves into sin. It took Jesus' death—an unbelievable price—to buy us back. Thus, for those who receive Him as Savior, we are twice owned.

We do not belong to ourselves; we have been bought with a price. That price was the blood of Christ. Rejoice at the willingness of Jesus to buy us back. With gratitude, give your life to Him in worship and service.

To be twice bought is to be forever owned.

Reflections/Prayer Requests

DAY 29

Ruth 4:12-13

"May your house be like the house of Perez, whom Tamar bore to Judah, because of the offspring which the Lord will give you from this young woman." So Boaz took Ruth and she became his wife; and when he went in to her, the Lord gave her conception, and she bore a son.

The Path to Fruitfulness

Fruitfulness doesn't just happen by chance. Some time ago, an agricultural school in Iowa reported that the production of 100 bushels of corn from one acre of land, in addition to the many hours of a farmer's labor, required four million gallons of water, 6,800 pounds of oxygen, 5,200 pounds of carbon, 160 pounds of nitrogen, 125 pounds of potassium, 75 pounds of yellow sulfur and other elements too numerous to list. It takes a lot of elements working together to produce fruitfulness.

Ruth discovered the same truth. Her life in Moab had been empty. The years of marriage with Naomi's son had been barren. But when she committed herself to the God of Israel, her life began to bear fruit. By faith she left her homeland and God gave her a new home. In simple trust she went out to the harvest fields, hoping to find someone who would allow her to glean after his reapers, and she found favor in the eyes of Boaz. Seeking to follow God's leading, she married Boaz and bore a son through whom the Messiah came to redeem the world. From a life of barrenness, God brought her, through faith, to great fruitfulness.

Faithfully trusting the Lord is still the only pathway to true fruitfulness. Jesus promised, "He who abides in Me, and I in him, bears much fruit." The world offers other options, but none result in lasting fruit. Only as we place our faith in Christ for daily guidance will we bear fruit for eternity.

Begin each day with reading God's Word. As He reveals His mind to you, faithfully obey everything you understand and ask for more wisdom when you don't. That's the way to bear fruit that will last forever.

Fruitfulness is the natural by-product of faithfulness.

Reflections/Prayer Requests

_____

_____

_____

_____

DAY 30

Then the women said to Naomi, "Blessed be the LORD, who has not left you this day without a close relative; and may his name be famous in Israel! And may he be to you a restorer of life and a nourisher of your old age; for your daughter-in-law, who loves you, who is better to you than seven sons, has borne him."

Better Than Seven Sons

A popular magazine carries a section in which it offers its readers the opportunity to send pictures of their part of the country and tell why they think it's the best. Month after month, people send in beautiful photos from all over the United States, and invariably someone will comment about their particular area, "It can't get any better than this."

That's what the women of Bethlehem were saying to Naomi. To have a son was wonderful. It was the responsibility of a Jewish son to care for his mother when his father passed away. He was her security and companion in old age. But these women agreed; Ruth was better than seven sons. She had done all that any son would have done and more—she had borne Naomi a grandson, the assurance that she would be taken care of in her latter years. It couldn't get any better than this.

This is also what Christ has done for us. Through His blood He has cleansed us from our sins. The past is forgiven. Through His Word we have the wisdom to live day by day. And through His Spirit we have the power to be His witnesses wherever we are. Through His resurrection we have the assurance that we, too, shall be raised beyond the grave to spend eternity in heaven. Everything is taken care of—past, present and future.

Have you thanked Jesus yet today for meeting your every need? There is nothing that can be added to what He has done and will do for you. It just can't get any better than this.

Only a complete Savior can make us complete.

Reflections/Prayer Requests

_____

_____

_____

_____

_____

_____

_____

DAY 31

Ruth 4:18-22

Now this is the genealogy of Perez: Perez begot Hezron; Hezron begot Ram, and Ram begot Amminadab; Amminadab begot Nahshon, and Nahshon begot Salmon; Salmon begot Boaz, and Boaz begot Obed; Obed begot Jesse, and Jesse begot David.

A Royal Pedigree

Scientists in London extracted a DNA sample from the skeleton of a man who supposedly was a Stone Age hunter-gatherer who lived 9,000 years ago. The specimen was then compared to DNA samples taken from individuals living in the same area. Much to his surprise, Adrian Targett, a British school teacher, discovered that his DNA was almost a perfect match. Researchers are claiming that this is the longest human lineage ever traced.

Ruth and Boaz may not be able to claim the longest lineage, but they can lay claim to the most royal one. Their ancestry stretched back to Perez, the son of Judah, the son of Abraham. It looked forward to such notables as Obed and Jesse and to the greatest king who ever ruled Israel, David. But it didn't stop there. Through a multitude of kings and others, the lineage of Ruth and Boaz can be traced unmistakably to Jesus Christ, the Messiah.

But Ruth and Boaz, with their impressive family tree, are not the only ones who can claim to be part of this most royal family. Paul wrote that Christ came "to redeem those who were under the law, that we might receive the adoption as sons" (Gal. 4:5). Every believer is adopted into the royal family through Jesus Christ. The apostle Peter said we are a "royal priesthood" (1 Pet. 2:9). We are the sons and daughters of God the Father (Eph. 1:5). We are even joint-heirs with Christ (Rom. 8:17).

If you have trusted Jesus Christ as your Savior, you are part of the royal family. You are a child of the King. Be proud of your lineage, and take care of the King's reputation. Do nothing that would disgrace the family name. Let your behavior be worthy of the royal family.

Being a member of the royal family brings great privileges—and great responsibility.

Reflections/Prayer Requests

_____

_____

_____

_____

_____

_____

GIANTS OF THE OLD TESTAMENT

Look for these other titles in the series:

Lessons on Living From Moses

Lessons on Living From Esther

Lessons on Living From Isaiah

Lessons on Living From Joshua

Lessons on Living From Abraham

Lessons on Living From Elijah

Also coming in 1998:

Lessons on Living From Jeremiah

Lessons on Living From David

Lessons on Living From Solomon

Lessons on Living From Daniel

Lessons on Living From Job

Lessons on Living From Joseph